BRIEFIN

D0680072

2·99

China

Glenn Myers

Authentic
LIFESTYLE

First published 2003 by Authentic Lifestyle

Authentic Lifestyle is an imprint of Authentic Media
PO Box 300, Carlisle, Cumbria CA3 0QS, UK
and PO Box 1047, Waynesboro, GA30830-2047 USA

08 07 06 05 04 03   7 6 5 4 3 2 1

British Library Cataloguing in Publication Data
A catalogue record for this book is available from the British Library

ISBN 1-85078-550-3

Designed by Christopher Lawther, Teamwork, Lancing, West Sussex.
Typeset by Profile, Rewe, Exeter, Devon.
Produced by Jeremy Mudditt Publishing Services, Carlisle,
and printed and bound in Great Britain by Printpoint, Bradford, W. Yorks.

CONTENTS

THANKS ....

This book was researched by a colleague who travelled across China, interviewed lots of people and gathered most of the material. Grateful thanks to her for doing all the heavy lifting. Many people supplied information and criticized early drafts of this book, improving it a lot. Thank you for your all your time and effort. The remaining mistakes, prejudices, and insensitivities are my own, and I'm sorry.

While we tried to collect all new material, I'd like to acknowledge my great debts to some of the people who have researched and written extensively about China already. Tony Lambert of OMF International, Paul Hattaway of Asia Harvest, Ross Paterson of Chinese Church Support Ministries and the materials produced by ChinaSource and Open Doors are vital sources for anyone who wants to learn more about China from a Christian perspective. I hope anyone who has had a taster of things in this *Briefing* will go on to explore their excellent resources.

And thanks to the regular team who have been in on this project from the outset: my colleagues at WEC International in the UK, my publisher Jeremy Mudditt and my wife and children.

Glenn Myers
October 2003

This book is produced by Wellspring Media, the UK media department of WEC International

WEC is an international, interdenominational missions agency aiming to bring the Christian gospel to the remaining unevangelized nations of the world. WEC currently has over 1750 workers from 43 nations serving Christ together in 60 countries.
www.wec-int.org.uk

– 1 –
The Middle Kingdom

IF ENGINEERS RULED THE EARTH

On the last day of December 2002, the ribbon was cut on a new railway. Resting on thin air 15 cm above a single rail, levitated by electromagnets, trains whip between the glittering skyscrapers to make the journey from Shanghai's Pudong Airport to Shanghai's railway station in just eight minutes. This is the world's first commercial 'maglev'—a showpiece in a city of showpieces.

It is no longer news that each year, China re-equips itself with more and more of the inventory of superpowerdom, restoring its place in the world, climbing once again to the heights.

China's national bird, so the joke goes, is the crane: at the height of its building boom Pudong was said to be home to one quarter of the entire world's flock. They are endemic in China now, patiently assembling shopping malls and apartment blocks.

The scale of construction is not for people of nervous disposition. China adds, for example, 3,000km of new expressway per year and 1,500km of new (conventional) railway. It is hoping to build 600 new cities in the first decade of this century. Other cities, it moves to make way for the Three Gorges scheme, the world's ultimate mega-dam project. The infrastructure for the 2008 Beijing Olympics is a statement of arrival as a world-class city. If you want to see what the whole world would be like if engineers ruled the earth (most of China's top leaders are engineers), come visit the Middle Kingdom—China's ancient name for itself—and gasp.

Every measure you can think of—infant mortality, carbon dioxide emissions, sales of soft beds, soft drinks, or soft toilet paper—records China's dramatic dash to reach developed-country standards, for good or ill. Economic growth and development in China is everything, the overriding national goal.

DENG FEVER

A developed China will be Deng Xiaoping's monument. One of the twentieth century's great figures, he assumed power in 1979 as an old man (after years of being alternately given high responsibility and then purged). But with characteristic boldness and brilliance, he scrapped the high road of Communist economics that his predecessor Mao Zedong preached, and set China on the grubby path to capitalism. Despite all the predictable bad that flowed out of this (corruption, greed, repression, inequality, pollution), no political leader in history has taken more people out of poverty than Deng.[1]

Deng's scrapping of Mao was done with due deference towards the old ancestor. Party doctrine claims it is still continuing in the course Mao set. Mao has a lavish Mausoleum (or perhaps a Maosoleum) in Tiananmen Square, and the old dictator's corpse is said to travel by lift each morning from a deep-freeze to the viewing chamber, before being reverently stowed back in the fridge each night. In the new China, even Mao commutes.

Jiang Zemin continued Deng's course after Deng's death in 1997[2], and Hu Jintao after him. Thus capitalism under Party control has now been pursued in China for about as long as Maoism was pursued before it. It has brought increasing prosperity throughout the country, a fantastic achievement—feeding 22% of

the world's population from only 8% of the world's farmland[3] for example, or becoming ever more like the manufacturing hub for all of planet earth.

China's re-emergence as a superpower, everyone seems to believe, will be one of the stories of the 21st century.

AND STILL MAO LOOKS DOWN

The pictures from Tiananmen Square on June 4th 1989—pro-democracy demonstrations smashed by tanks—were one of the motifs of the late 20th century. Communist structures were crumbling like cheap concrete in Russia, Eastern Europe, and Central Asia, but in China, it was Orwellian business-as-usual: the 'People's Republic' deployed the 'People's Liberation Army' to crush the people's liberation movement.

In this, the Chinese government under Deng was restating an old theme. China may now be economically liberal. But China's leaders have always had absolute power, and in that sense nothing has changed over several thousand years.

Political control, 21st century style, means, for example:[4] Internet access is being promoted across China but connection to the global internet is policed. Newspapers in China have changed dramatically in recent years, and are full of colour, variety, profiles of pop stars, advertising—everything except original, informed, critical reportage. In 2002, Party circulars warned editors off 'stories related to central leaders and their families ... Taiwan, Tibet, and East Turkestan independence; religious extremists and Falungong; the military; social stratification; the south-north water diversion project; advocacy of private ownership; taxes and fees in rural areas; student loans; human genetic research; private entrepreneurs as Party delegates; lawsuits against the government; villagers who sold blood; *Forbes* ranking lists; Confucian moral education in primary schools; university rankings; the Qinghai-Tibet railroad; and major accidents.'[5] When *Securities Market Weekly* ran a story on how rich National People's Congress President Li Peng and his family had become, every issue was confiscated.

In stable times China never has had the alternative sources of power that in other countries are provided by warlords, parliaments, free presses, or labour or religious movements. Political opposition is still treated as 'dissent.' Anything that could serve as a means to mobilise people—religion, newspapers, political movements, campaigning organizations—are policed, sometimes crushed, by a state whose instincts are always to control.

Even more surprising to the outside observer, the people seem to accept all this. In its overriding fear of instability and chaos, the government reflects what the bulk of the people themselves seem to believe. It has concentrated on rice, not freedom, and most Chinese people have concluded that if you have to have one overriding priority—well, you can't eat freedom.

So even without strong political control, self-restraint and self-censorship would be the norm in China. This is not an instinctively open, confrontational, critical society. It's a cautious, protective, harmony-loving society. Part of the reason, for example, the SARS virus took hold in China in early 2003 was not 'government repression' but the instinctive desire, at every level, to keep bad news within the family, save embarrassment, and put on a good face to people outside.

THE STORY BEHIND THE STORY

This quiet, industrious, long-suffering approach to nation-building is worth looking at a little deeper. What powers this rise—mass starvation to maglevs in half a century? Why this willingness to take casualties and accept big restrictions in the headlong dash to prosperity? It may be helpful to see it all as a pointer to the Chinese outlook on the world. Crassly generalizing though we may be, here are a few tentative themes:[6]

1. *Greatness:* To be Chinese is to belong to one of the great cultures. No civilisation has climbed higher than the heights of China's art, literature, technology, philosophy, architecture. The list of China's traditional exports is a catalogue, in the Western folk-memory, of the most exquisite luxuries: silk, jade, porcelain.

2. *National pride:* For the past 150 years, the Chinese have had to endure terrible scenes. Imagine if this was your nation's recent past: military defeat, foreign domination, poverty, invasion, civil war, warlordism, dictatorship, starvation, mob violence and mass murder. Any nation would be passionate about regaining its lost pride: China—a major culture, and a culture governed by ideas of shame and honour—is so supremely, and rightly.

3. *Shortage:* Hunger, or the folk memory of it, also tugs at the robes. Through the millennia in China there has never been enough to go round. There have been comfortable, luxurious lives available for a few; hard, bitter and deprived lives for everyone else. China is not a culture where you wait in line, in the confident hope that there is enough for everyone. China is a culture where you jostle to get what you can when you can.

4. *Family:* The strategy for survival has always been: (1) Rely on a close web of relationships, supremely your family. (2) Make the most of any opportunity that any family member can grab.

China is a nation that deeply embraces the principle of self-sacrifice for the greater good. Grandparents take extra jobs to buy weekend tuition for the grandchild, the passport to a job. A young mum may leave her children with her in-laws for a couple of years so that she can take a promotion in her company. She won't do this for personal career fulfillment: as a member of the extended family on whom fortune has smiled, it is her duty to grab the chance on behalf of all.

China currently attracts a lion's share of foreign investment in the world. Partly this is because China is at the moment the biggest low-wage, business-friendly country on earth. But partly it is because of self-sacrifice and opportunity-seizing on a national scale.

5. *Obedience and conformity:* If you rely on a network of relationships for your welfare, you also have strict obligations to that network. There is a strong cultural value in China of children being 'filial' which implies putting up with, obeying, submitting to, honouring, and making prosperous the retirement of, the previous generations. It is—it could be argued—a lot nearer the Biblical ideal than the Western world's habit of abandoning the elderly to loneliness and government welfare.

This principle extends out through the culture. China is not a nation of brilliant individualists, mavericks who overthrow the status quo. Chinese art often depicts tiny people set against vast landscapes: *what are individuals after all?* it silently asks.[7]

Leadership (and followership) throughout the culture reflect what Chinese people learn at their mothers' or grandmothers' knees about how families work. Dissent is feared and rebuked, not encouraged. Rulers rule. Followers pull together, and if necessary, suffer silently or 'eat bitterness'. It is uncultural to defy family, question teachers, criticise the government: a free press is a threat to stability, a crack in the national foundations—not a sign of their strength and flexibility.

China has always had autocratic leaders and has usually had quiescent followers: that principle built the Great Wall and the Grand Canal in the past and is today building and pushing millions of people out of their homes and flooding the Three Gorges—self-sacrifice at the command of autocratic rulers, for the national good.

ONLY SO FAR

All of this takes us only so far. A land of 1.3 billion is vast and complex enough for every generalization to be proven both true and false. It is also changing, and staying the same. China overflows all analysis.

It is a land both conservative and mini-skirted; capitalist and entrepreneurial and nostalgic for socialism; it has cities of glittering office blocks and cities where, through the smog, you can view the grey lines of obsolete factories and unemployed workers. It has young children rendered myopic and obese by too much study and too many burgers; old people lean and scarred from a lifetime of hardship. It has baby girls left to die in woods; and mostly, it has masses of people muddling through. China is developing fast, but it has a vast, undeveloped hinterland. China's government attempts to control, but it is itself huge, unwieldy, uncontrolled.

And it is, of course, changing, rapidly (but also slowly)—evolving in ways no-one can predict. Expect everything, then expect the unexpected as well.

DENG FEVER AND THE CHURCH

The changes since Deng have had enormous consequences for the Church—which is the story of this book. There are many ways to understand the Church in China: a sovereign work of God, for example, or a miracle-seeking mass-movement such as always happens among peasants during an era of upheaval and powerlessness (as some Western journalists and anthropologists have claimed[8]). Let's start by looking back—in China, this means a *long* way back.

THE WILD FRONTIERS OF CAPITALISM

Numerous tragedies unfold on the grubby road to capitalism. Here are some samples:

- In the early 1990s the government set up 200 blood-donation stations in rural China, offering farmers 40 yuan (about £3) each time. Local government TV adverts recommended selling blood as the 'road to prosperity', and a valuable supplement to farm incomes. But health and safety provisions were skimped, syringes reused, equipment not sterilized. AIDS flourished, emptying whole villages. In 1996, the government closed the centres down, but illegal mobile ones arrived to fill the gap.[9]

- The bid for the 2000 Olympics brought out the worst in China while simultaneously trying to demonstrate the best to the world. In one horrific case, a harmless mentally handicapped man named Wang Chaoru was dragged from his home by the police lest he wander the streets and spoil the view for the Olympic Committee as they toured Beijing in 1993. After the Olympic Committee left, his parents were invited to collect his body, which had been beaten to death. They were later given a bag of money to keep quiet.[10] China lost the Olympic bid by one vote and the millennium games went to Sydney.

- One of Communism's extraordinary early achievements in the early 1950s was to end the plague of opium addiction that had dogged China for more than a century. And China stayed largely drug-free for several decades, despite sharing a large border with the world's leading heroin producers. But as Deng's reforms took hold in the late 1980s, the drug trade made its way into China via the south-west of the country, and drug addiction once more became a serious issue; even on official figures the number of Chinese addicts passed 1m in 2002.[11]

– 2 –
The view back

Just like when you look between two mirrors that face each other, China's history stretches backwards out of sight, but along the way you see the same images repeating.

Chinese civilisation first grew up in the fertile plains around the Yellow River; and like the other three river-valley civilisations of far antiquity (around the Nile, the Tigris/Euphrates, and the Ganges) it rose spontaneously and owed nothing to the others.

China's first cities were being built around the same time that, half a world away, Abraham was saddling his donkeys for the trip to Canaan. The first Chinese dynasty known to archaeology were the Shang: they were in power when baby Moses was being fished out of the Nile and were still in power when a doddery King David was handing rule over to Solomon.

Even as early as these Shang times, civilisation already had Chinese characteristics. You could identify a strong central control, for example, and clear divisions in society between, say, civil servants, and peasants. After the Shang dynasty fell, another feature of Chinese history became apparent: a period of division, chaos, and warfare until some new unifying dynasty arose.

The sage Confucius appeared on the scene in the 6th and 5th centuries BC—after the great Hebrew prophets, before the Greek philosophers, around about the time of Cyrus the Great. Confucius was a civil servant and scholar rather than a religious figure: he wasn't worshipped until centuries after his death. His teaching, and that of his near contemporary Laozi, the founder of 'Daoism', shape Chinese thought to this day.

These elements in place, the great scroll of Chinese history unrolled. In the strong dynasties, populations grew, colossal public works were done, regions like Tibet and Central Asia were colonized or otherwise dominated. For the best part of two thousand years, on and off, the Civil Service Examination System offered wealth, security and power to geekish kids who could reproduce Confucian lore to order. Chinese kids (of a certain social class) were being leveraged into top schools, drilled by tutors, and nagged to do their homework by Chinese mothers while kids of almost every other nation were still learning how to dig up roots or herd sheep. Chinese commitment to education goes deep.

Study the past, if you would divine the future — Confucius

In between the strong dynasties, population growth stagnated, sometimes there were terrible wars, and often there was great individual creativity which would only be fully harnessed by the next major dynasty.

TWO EMPIRES

It's easy in the West to forget China's place in world history. When Rome was at its height—say between 200BC and 200AD—so was a great Chinese civilisation under a series of dynasties dominated by the Han. Emperor Augustus took a census of his Roman Empire around 4BC, causing significant inconvenience to the world's only pregnant virgin. Six years later, his equivalent in China took an equally impressive census of his empire, and counted 57 million subjects.

Christ happened to be born in one of these great empires. How soon did the news travel to the other? Rome and Han China knew of each other, and swapped goods including Chinese silk via the Parthian empire.[12] It's intriguing to wonder if in that earliest era of East/West trade, the gospel also made the trip. There is no compelling evidence, despite some traditions of Chinese journeys of the apostles Thomas and Bartholomew.

But who knows what archaeology may turn up: a Christian apologist named Arnobius claimed around 305AD that the gospel had already found a response among the Chinese. Alas, he died leaving no footnotes.

ATTEMPT#1

Among the earliest records so far unearthed are a seventh century monastery near Xi'an,[13] some Christian graves in the far north-west, and the remarkable and justly famous 'Nestorian Stone', a granite slab erected to commemorate early missionaries from that Eastern denomination:

> There was in Syria a bishop named A-lo-pen ... He rode through hardship and danger, and in the ninth year of Cheng-Kuan arrived at Ch'ang-an ... The Emperor received him as guest in the palace. The Scriptures were translated in the imperial library, and their doctrine examined by the Emperor himself. Knowing full well that it was right and true he expressly commanded its propagation.[14]

Alopen's mission dated from 635 AD—the same time that Irish monks like Columba and Aiden were evangelizing Britain. Under the great T'ang dynasty Alopen's monks prospered. They produced China's first recorded Christian books, copies of which were re-discovered in the early 20th century. There is some doubt as to how far their Christian faith escaped the monasteries and impacted the land. But they provided Christian testimony near China's capital for more than two centuries.

In 907, the T'ang dynasty ended in peasant revolts. China dissolved from one into ten states, and the Christian faith appears not to have survived the regime-change—leaving the impression that the Nestorian mission of Alopen had relied more on imperial patronage than grass-roots strength.

ATTEMPT #2

In 987 a team of monks was sent to investigate the state of the church in China and found nothing.[15] A pity: under a new dynasty, China was prospering, developing the inventions for which it later became famous (block printing, porcelain-making, navigation by compass and also banking and property innovations). The new capital, Hanzhou, was the greatest city on earth—and, so far as we know, quite beyond the realm of Christian witness.

Meanwhile, Nestorianism survived among the non-Chinese tribes to the north and west of the Great Wall. When Genghis Khan first united some of these tribes and then charged off to all quarters conquering the earth, Nestorianism came along in the baggage. The Mongols advanced on China for most of the thirteenth century, completing their conquest under Kublai Khan in 1287. Kublai used Nestorians as advisors and civil servants, and with them, Christianity returned to the Middle Kingdom.

Three years later, as the Western world began to enlarge its horizons, Catholicism joined in, under the solitary and heroic figure of John of Montecorvino, a Franciscan friar. This remarkable missionary sailed to what is now Beijing via India, built two churches in the capital, and by 1305 reported 6,000 converts. In a letter home he noted, 'I have already grown old, and my hair is white from the labours and tribulations.'[16] Further Franciscans followed, and the work spread to several cities.

As with the previous Christian witness in China, however, the Franciscan work failed to survive a regime-change. A bishop was killed in a nationalist uprising; the Ming dynasty replaced the foreign-based Yuan (Mongol) dynasty; and Christians were expelled from Beijing. In the isolationist Ming times, neither Catholicism nor Nestorianism were allowed a foothold—and so, probably, the second instance of bringing news of Christ to China ended.

ATTEMPT #3

Fast forward to the end of the Ming dynasty—late 16th century—before Catholics successfully tried again. (In the interim, Nestorianism had virtually disappeared as a force on the earth).[17]

Catholic ministry in China had two faces—one that the authorities approved of, and one that they didn't—not unlike today. Scholarly Jesuits, particularly the brilliant Matteo Ricci and Michele de Ruggieri, aimed to reach the elite. They studied Chinese classical texts, trying to explain the Christian faith in Chinese terms. They used Western technology and learning (in this case, clockmaking, astronomy and mathematics) to gain a welcome in the emperor's court and thus, they hoped, earn a hearing for the gospel in the Imperial Ear. They accepted compromises in order to keep their position—compromises that the authorities in Rome thought were far too far. And they saw over 500 members of the Ming court itself embrace Christianity.

Starting a little later, other Catholic missionaries began trying to reach the poor in the villages. They met folk religion rather than high philosophy and had to adjust their teaching accordingly. They saw thousands of converts, were not well-respected by the authorities, and were persecuted. To add to the complications, Rome kept weighing in with rulings that annoyed the emperors and hampered the Christian workers—an early example of unhelpful Western interference in Chinese business.

In 1724, the emperor ordered all the Christians to renounce their faith, and all the missionaries to leave, except the handful of Jesuits who worked at the State Bureau of Astronomy.

The Catholic Church of the villages was forced underground, where, run largely by women, and away from Papal intervention, it lived on. There were still 200,000 of these underground Catholics in China by 1750.[18]

ATTEMPT #3 (CONTINUED)

All was to change in the nineteenth century.

In 1800, China's happy sense of superpowerdom and invincibility was intact. This was the Middle Kingdom, ancient centre and home of civilisation. When Westerners came offering items for trade, emperors received them as bringing tribute from fawning, distant isles. In any case, China saw little need for inferior foreign produce.

Nor did they feel the need for foreign religions. Robert Morrison, first Protestant missionary to China, scrabbled on the threshold of China for years from 1807, not at all welcome as a Bible translator. His linguistic brilliance, however, earned him a job with the British East India Company, and in his spare time, in conditions of total secrecy and some danger, he translated the entire Bible.[19] Morrison's two Chinese tutors carried poison

DR. MORRISON STUDYING THE CHINESE LANGUAGE.

with them, so that, if caught, they could commit suicide rather than suffer a tedious valedictory in the Imperial torture chambers.[20]

Morrison's work was desperately hard. He saw just ten Chinese commit their lives to Christ in his 27 years as a missionary. When his first child died, he was not allowed to bury him on Chinese soil. The costs were similar for the other early pioneers. Nothing but their faith told them that enormous changes were coming.

The year 1839 is a suitable milestone. China's exports, especially tea, were finding a large and expanding market in the West. To stop this one-way flow of capital, the British had the bright idea of selling goods from their colonies to China—raw cotton, which was useful, and opium, which was anything but. To fund their tea-drinking habits, then, the British became drug-pushers-in-chief to the Chinese Empire.

Opium was an illegal drug in China, for all the same reasons it is illegal today. In 1839, the emperor sent his emissary—an early drug czar in an early war on drugs—to the port of Guangzhou. He detained the entire foreign community and seized thousands of chests of opium. The British, anxious to protect the trade with India, found a reason to go to war and to their enormous surprise and lasting humiliation, the Chinese were defeated.

Then they were forced to make many concessions towards opening up their country to foreign trade, and fined (or robbed, depending on your point of view). The opium trade strengthened: China weakened. Other Western powers piled in, demanding similar rights. So began a century of humiliation and Western crime that still casts a long shadow over the Middle Kingdom.

Just as when Genghis Khan breached the Great Wall and invaded China in the thirteenth century, so in the nineteenth: missionaries came along with the conquerors—an uncomfortable alliance. One can imagine what captains of opium ships thought when they found that their paying passengers were mostly hymn-singing Christian workers, anxious about the state of the captain's soul.

If the missionaries had an uneasy relationship with the conquerors, they were equally at risk from the conquered: once in China the missionaries were sometimes thousands of miles inland, isolated and vulnerable. Often, they were the only 'Western' presence in town and however much they adopted Chinese dress, they could not escape their Western origin.

It was awkward, unsatisfactory, dangerous, easy to criticize and it was amazing they could achieve anything—yet they came, and did achieve. Prime among them was James Hudson Taylor with his radical, controversial, China Inland Mission.

The CIM, famously, was born on the Sunday morning of June 25th, 1865, on the pebbles of Brighton beach, in southern England. After months of mental anguish, Taylor came to a point where he asked and trusted God for two workers for each of China's twelve interior provinces—workers funded without appeals for finance, renouncing colonial dress and manners, taking up hazardous positions in the far interior, with only God to depend on for safety. Taylor sent committed Christians of any Protestant denomination, and he was happy to send single women.

Taylor said he based his life on three facts: *There is a living God. He has spoken in the Bible. He means what he says and he will do all he has promised.* His simplicity and vision had the marks of God about them and struck a deep chord. By the time of Taylor's death in 1905 the CIM had 849 workers and had acted as midwife for 125,000 Chinese Protestant Christians, all over China. Thousands of missionaries of other societies also worked in the country, many basing themselves on CIM principles.

More than anyone, these pioneers laid the foundations for the great, indigenous Chinese Church we see today.

AND THE DYNASTIES CHANGE

The nineteenth-century encounter with the West toppled the ruling dynasty and led to some years of violence and chaos before a new political order arose. These were awful times of revolt and counter-revolt, good times not to be born in, times of a nation swinging between tradition and modernity, its ancient structures collapsing further with each swing.

First came the pseudo-Christian Taiping Rebellion (pro-modern, anti-emperor), which may have cost 40 million lives, a nightmare conflict whose proportions completely overshadow the American Civil War, which happened at much the same time. Chinese leaders today still fear the combustible mixture of peasants and Christian-type movements, in a failing state.

In 1899-1900 the Boxer Rebellion (anti-modern, pro-emperor), swept away the lives of perhaps 50,000 Chinese Christians and nearly 200 from the missionary community—not the worst massacre of Christians but easily the worst massacre of Protestant missionaries in all history.

The twentieth century brought more years of war, famine, humiliation, failed reform and chaos—and incidentally, very fruitful years for the

Church. Large, independent, indigenous Chinese Churches began to be established in the 1920s and 1930s.

Communist China was established in 1949, to the relief of many. Communism, we can easily forget, was touted as a short-cut to modernity and prosperity, a flat-pack solution for failing peasant states, so it too was pro-modern, and anti-emperor.

PASSION WEEK, AND WHAT FOLLOWED

Communism was murderous on Church and nation, scarring those it didn't kill. Mao Zedong was a true believer. He believed in the ideology (class struggle, communal ownership) and insisted on the forcible conversion of unbelievers through re-education or persecution.

The Party was popular at first. Party members were well-ordered, idealistic, and much less corrupt than the officials they were replacing. They were fighting for the poor and for the peasants against the warlords and the landlords. They offered radical change and new hope. And some of the Communist policies worked well, especially where they helped small communities to co-operate and so work their farms more efficiently. Communism also brought a revolution in education and health care, and as we have seen, largely ended the opium problem.

But these great gains were eclipsed and lost, overrun by human sin, the

absolute power of the Party leading to the near-absolute ruin of the nation. Mao was the 'Great Helmsman' who piloted this greatest of nations with military precision and at full speed straight onto the rocks. His 'Hundred Flowers Campaign' (let many opinions bloom, like a hundred flowers on the hillside) led inevitably to severe repression of all free thought and debate; his 'Great Leap Forward' plunged China back into mass starvation worthy of mediaeval times; his 'Cultural Revolution' attempted to destroy everything good, worthy and noble that Chinese culture had ever nurtured.

The Church suffered fully as much as anyone, driven underground, its leaders exiled to nightmarish labour camps or simply killed.

Mao's contribution, then, was thoroughly to prepare for a resurrection.

– 3 –
Resurrection

For a resurrection, you need a death. Pick a date like 1969, and the Church really did seem like the 'valley of dry bones' of Ezekiel's vision.[21]

Essentially nothing was left standing. Church buildings were being reused by the State as warehouses or kindergartens. Christian leaders were working out thirty- and forty-year sentences of hard labour. (One later calculated he had personally pushed 200,000 underground coal trucks). Even the neutered, Communist-controlled, Three-Self Patriotic Movement, a 1950s invention that was at best a sickly shadow of a Church, had been decapitated. There was not a single visible congregation of Chinese Christians in the entire country.

Yet a little more than thirty years later, in the same country, as is now well-documented, China has a large, thriving, public, richly varied Church. In the most favoured counties, 15% or more of the population are registered as Christians, and every kilometre you travel brings you to another church.[22] In a few of the tribal areas, 50% or more of the population is officially Christian.

How big is the Church in total? That's hotly contested, with one part of the Church damping down the figures while another pumps them up.

The official number of adult Protestants in registered churches is, say, 17m. (The official figures vary). On top of that are children, Catholics, and unregistered Christians.

Other equally-official statistics say that there have been 30m Bibles legally published since 1986.[23] Let's guess that 10 million more have been smuggled in or clandestinely printed, and yet there is still, in rural areas, a shortage of Bibles.[24] One Bible smuggler said to us: 'There have been articles in some Bible Society publications stating there is no need to import or smuggle Bibles … I found in my experience quite the opposite is the case.'[25] As late as 2000, United Bible Societies themselves (who help with the official supply of Bibles) were talking about rural communities where 100 people share a single Bible.[26] So China has absorbed perhaps 40m Bibles in the past 15 years and is still short.

The prayer handbook *Operation World*, synthesizing all the available claims and counter-claims, records a range of estimates for the Christian community from '30m-150m',[27] which shows what a hopeless task counting sheep in China is.

What is certainly true is that the pre-revolution figure of a 1.8m Protestant community[28] has multiplied twenty-fold or more in one generation—perhaps much more. This would be remarkable in a small jungle tribe. In a continent-sized country that accounts for a fifth of all the human beings in existence, it is world-shaking.

HOW IT HAPPENED

This growth didn't happen because of brilliant missiology, careful application of church growth principles, or even from reading other titles in the *Briefings* series. Here are what seem to be the ingredients.

Prayer: For a couple of decades in the 20th century, just about all the Church worldwide could do, in or out of China, was pray. And many groups and agencies, and many individuals, kept on faithfully wielding this single spiritual weapon. No-one can calculate the effect of this, but given what's happened since, it doesn't look like too bad a strategy.

Foundations: One hundred and fifty years of Protestant missionary work (and 300 years of Catholic work) had put in place a Christian infrastructure: Bibles, church leaders, churches, training facilities, some modelling of what Christianity can look like in a Chinese context. Behind those visible achievements were the intangible years of preaching, praying, and living and suffering for Jesus. Many seeds had fallen into the ground and died. The ground which looked so bare, it turns out, was actually littered with fallen seed.

At the same time, China was being wrecked: first, ancient foundations were wearing out; second, Communist cowboy builders were in charge of repairs. All this, shall we say, encouraged a certain openness to new solutions.

Communications: The Communists wrapped China in roads and railways, taught the people to read, and made the Mandarin dialect the national language, all of which has helped the gospel to spread.

A Church criminalized: The Communists felt that the Christian Church could offer a real alternative to the Party's hold on power. So it came under systematic attack. Normal, Biblical Christianity was criminalized. One effect of this was to make Chinese Christians deadly serious about their faith. People do not spend 20 years in a labour camp in defence of a hobby.

The Church suffered with the nation: Communism established one sort of equality in China: everyone suffered.

It is tempting to think that one of the reasons the Church has so bloomed in the last several decades is because in the darkest times the Christians suffered along with the rest, but somehow did so with more purpose, meaning, and grace: the light shone in the darkness. This suffering also killed the assumption that Chinese Christians were Christians because of the perks that come from foreigners. Suffering authenticated and indigenised the Church.

A vacuum: What was left after Mao was a vacuum. Deng Xiaoping led China to embrace capitalism. But neither he nor his successors have offered anything for the soul. Greed is the new righteousness in many quarters. Since ancient traditions have been bulldozed, and 'Marxist-Leninist-Mao-Zedong Thought' is discredited, the ground has been cleared for ideologies old and new.

The gospel: Chinese Christianity is founded on preaching the crucified, risen Christ, who saves from sin all who come to Him in repentance and faith. It's an uncompromisingly Biblical faith. Chinese Christianity is recognizably and definitively a gospel movement. The Chinese Church has the genetic code of true churches everywhere and is thus hard to kill off.

A measure of religious freedom restored: Religious freedoms in China are still restricted, mostly by the arbitrariness of local officials. But since Deng, the Church has been given some room to grow. The Church has made the most of these freedoms, and has even, by its vigour, created ever more space for itself.

Christian love: Many times, the Church has offered people authentic love and acceptance, a powerful testimony in any culture.

The supernatural: Christianity has grown on the back of the supernatural. This much is agreed. Healings and miracles are common in the Chinese Church, and they have attracted and convinced many people, including high officials, to turn to Christ.

How you explain all these phenomena depends to some extent on the worldview you start with. People who find miracles hard to stomach suggest explanations like the mass hysteria of gullible peasants in uncertain times. This is surely a factor (it also helps explain the rise of other miracle-working movements, such as the Qigong philosophy of spiritual power that is said to influence even the highest ranks of Chinese leadership). But Christians would say that such arguments don't account for all the facts: God's sovereignty plays a part too.

Everyone agrees that it is not by many clever words that the Chinese Church has grown: it is by clearly perceived spiritual power.

– 4 –
What it's like now

If we took a snapshot of the Chinese Church at the beginning of the third Christian millennium, what would we see? We'd have to look at both an official, and an unofficial, Christian movement.

1. THE OFFICIAL CHURCH

China's state-approved Christian body is the so-called 'Three-Self Patriotic Movement' or TSPM. The 'Three-Self' principles reflected the best mission principles of the day: a truly Chinese Church—self-govern-ing, self-supporting and self-propa-gating—was what the missionaries themselves had been aiming for.

Here's an official account of how the TSPM came into being, from the for-mer TSPM chairman, Luo Guanzhong:[29]

> *Since 1840 until the establishment of the New China, imperialism had all along used Christianity and missionaries to serve aggression, and they have never stopped. In the fifties, through the Chinese Three-Self Patriotic Movement, China's Christians for the first time stood up and, with their new political stance, unmasked the connection between the Western missionary movement in China and the imperialist aggression against China.*

The State helped to shape the thinking of China's Christians, it must be added, by expelling foreign missionaries, banning denominations, and referring anyone with questions or comments to the labour camps.

From the beginning, the 'Three-Self' movement looked less like a spontaneous act of liberation by Chinese Christians and more like a Communist Party attempt to tame the Protestant Church and re-educate it until it withered and died. (Parallel organizations were set up for the Catholics, Buddhists, Daoists, and Muslims.)

Its structure demonstrated this:

1. At every level, the TSPM was under direct Party control: local branches of the TSPM reported to local branches of the Party, regional branches to regional branches, and so on. The Party thus had a close-up view and a veto of all TSPM actions. Local Party branches could, for example, stop churches being built or forbid certain people to preach.

2. The Party only allowed a TSPM leadership that was 'Patriotic' (loyal to the Party). This tended to mean theological liberals or even Party members (never mind that they were atheists).

3. The Party severely restricted church activity by forbidding much of it, licensing the rest, and then being stingy with the licences.

In the late 1950s and early 1960s Party control was so obvious that it convinced no-one. Tony Lambert tells of churches that were 'empty of all save a faithful remnant of the elderly and a coterie of politically motivated church leaders whose leadership shaded into total and abject collaboration with the Party.'[30]

THE TSPM IS NOT A TAME CHURCH

Fifty years on, any number of 'self-governing, self-supporting and self-propagating' Chinese Christian movements have been created—the unregistered churches. And the TSPM itself has, year by year, become less of a state puppet and more like a true Church of Jesus Christ. You could say, by the grace of God and the faithfulness of Chinese Christians, the TSPM, as a policy instrument for extending the rule of the Communist Party has failed. As an instrument for extending the Kingdom of God, however, it seems to have succeeded quite well.

What do we make of the TSPM Church today? As with everything else in China, we have several stories going on in parallel, and the 'real' story happens somewhere in between. (It also helps to distinguish between the largely liberal TSPM leadership and the TSPM churches which, at the grassroots, are overwhelmingly evangelical.)

Story one: the TSPM as Established Church. Millions of evangelicals happily worship within the TSPM. Half a million new Christians are baptized into it every year. New meeting points open every Sunday. It trains leaders. It prints Bibles. It has an extensive and growing ministry of social action that is reaching into truly needy areas of Chinese life. Its theologians travel to foreign seminaries for academic text-wrestling sessions, just like the theologians of other churches.

In short, the TSPM is like established or state Protestant churches the world over: flawed and fallen, often with the wrong people in high office, a little too fond of the perks that come from a cosy relationship with the state, yet with all that, a genuinely spiritual character.

Story two: the TSPM as a corrupt church. The plague of corruption that is sweeping all of China is certainly also found in the TSPM.

For example, the leaders of Trinity Church in Kunming collected six million yuan from worshippers for a new church building. All they have to show is a demolished former church building (the site was sold to developers) and a luxury apartment block for the hardworking Three-Self pastors. The six million yuan is all spent.[31]

In another example, the official church magazine *Tian Feng* described how someone who couldn't recite a single line of the Lord's Prayer was first baptized, then ultimately elected as a county TSPM head, by using connections in the Religious Affairs Bureau.[32]

Story three: the TSPM as enemy of the unregistered churches. There is an element of the TSPM that hates the unregistered churches.

Some members of TSPM churches work as government informers, reporting on unregistered church activities. Top TSPM leadership is quick to write off many of the unregistered Christians as cults, condemn Bible smuggling as 'infiltration', and downplay the size of the unregistered church. In all this, they lend support to the most paranoid, violent and repressive face of China.

Story four: TSPM as a missionary movement. The TSPM has no taste for making grand statements of missionary vision, or bold plans to evangelise the nation and the world. In fact, officially at least, they rather despise all that kind of talk.

Yet, quietly, and without much fuss, the TSPM has won victory after victory for Christianity in China. TSPM Christians move mountains, by faith, a spadeful at a time. Some examples:

- At a major workshop on government religious policy in 2001, then-President Jiang Zemin quietly conceded that the Church was not going to wither away quickly.[33] The subtext? The Communist Party has tried to eradicate the Church, and it has completely failed, the battle is lost. Nowadays the Church shows much more health and vigour, and recruits more members each year, than the Party does.

- Christianity is now part of mainstream Chinese life. Churches are open, publicly available, for all to see. Christians have been named, many times, as model citizens. Christians are earning great respect through their hard work, their love, their care for the needy. This is the direct result of millions of acts of faithfulness of TSPM Christians and it has removed for ever the stigma that Christianity had throughout the missionary era, of being foreign, marginal, an unChinese activity. It's a massive achievement.

- TSPM resources find their way into the unregistered churches, whether it is Bibles or trained personnel, so the whole Christian movement is strengthened.

- Many, many Christians belong both to the TSPM and the unregistered churches, and take the best from both. The TSPM thus becomes one of the pillars of Chinese church life, which, like a trellis, helps support the  growth of the unregistered movement.

And TSPM people keep pushing at the boundaries. Some TSPM Christians have a habit of breaking China's restrictive religion laws, and seeing what happens.

For example, it is still illegal to hold Sunday Schools for children, yet some TSPM churches openly hold Sunday Schools or youth fellowships. Some such church groups have been described, in glowing terms, in recent government-approved press releases.[34]

Once that kind of precedent is established, it becomes ever harder for a local official to send in the Public Security Bureau to snap the crayons, tip the orange juice on the floor and frogmarch the Sunday School teachers to a labour camp. China is proud of the TSPM's freedoms, and the prouder China is of them, the freer and bolder the TSPM gets. And so when many of the TSPM local leaders steadfastly break the rules, it is not surprising that officials quietly look the other way.

'In a very Chinese way,' points out Tony Lambert, '[Chinese Christians] are subverting the system which has been set up to subvert the church.'[35]

2. THE NON-OFFICIAL CHURCHES

The unofficial Christian movement includes everything that is outside of the Three-Self world. They usually meet in buildings other than church buildings (or in the open air), hence their 'house-church' label. In some places they can meet openly and publicly, in others they still keep hidden.

Some characteristics:

Exuberantly alive. Unregistered churches are found throughout the country, and they are still growing. Many of them network together, but the whole picture is too complex to grasp—a tangled jungle of rampant

growth. Missions researcher Paul Hattaway compares them to a glop of spaghetti on a plate. You can perceive various strands, but how they all fit together, and where one ends and another begins, is beyond even guesswork.

Most observers seem to think there are many more unregistered Christians than there are registered Christians. Even the government concedes there are 17m TSPM Christians; there must be tens of millions of unregistered believers. *Operation World's* guess of an unregistered Protestant Christian community of 42m in 2000 is probably a fair synthesis of the available data. But expect that figure to be revised drastically—upwards or downwards.[36]

However the statistics play out, nobody questions the overall story: there are millions and millions of Chinese believers, far more than official figures suggest. After missionary attempts stretching back 1500 years, the Christian Church is at last widely spread and deeply rooted in China. For most of Christian history the Chinese have been under-represented in the global Church. Now they are here at last, in numbers, and by their life and suffering are reminding all the rest of us how high Christ's standards are.

Rural and urban. In the 1980s Chinese Christianity was based in the countryside (no bad thing, since China itself is still a village-based, rural country, though perhaps it may not be for many decades longer.) After the crushing of the 1989 pro-democracy movement, however, Christianity began to be embraced in large numbers by students and 'intellectuals'.

Some Chinese Christian leaders have calculated that a city like Beijing now has half a million Christians.[37] Others dispute these figures. But again it shows that Christian leaders believe even the national capital is being infected by Christianity fever.

Evangelical. Chinese house-church Christians preach, study and believe in the Bible.

They have the problems and blessings of *youth and life*. So there is fast growth, great vision and zeal; there is also misuse of statistics and power; schism and scandal; legalism; power seeking; and various theological peculiarities that are defended with unholy passion.

Unregistered Christians are still *persecuted*. The picture varies over the whole country, depending on many factors such as the willingness or otherwise of local officials to turn a blind eye. The cities are freer than the countryside. In most cases, 'persecution' is really about low-level intimidation and harassment. But still today, local security forces will break up Christian meetings, confiscate books and video-discs, impose heavy fines on Christians and imprison them, and beat and humiliate them with electric batons. This happens to hundreds of Christians each year.

STAYING OUT ...

Why do the churches stay outside the TSPM? Several reasons:

- In many areas of China, Party restrictions on Christianity are so restrictive and heavy-handed that many Christians find it impossible to register. Some churches have only registered after hundreds of representations to the authorities. This is especially true in the countryside, where some Communist Party cadres are still faithfully banging the drum for the old Chairman.

- In some places local TSPM leaders may be so out of step with the beliefs of ordinary Christians that it may seem pointless or even contrary to the spirit of the New Testament to sit under their ministry or have fellowship with them.

- Some house-church Christians have objections in principle to belonging to any kind of state-sponsored church, or have objections to the teaching that comes from the highest levels of TSPM leadership. As with many state churches around the world, TSPM leadership belongs more to the world of politics than to the world of the ordinary church member.

- Some don't like the theology and worship culture of their local TSPM churches.

- Some—in the most liberal, urban settings—are not aware that their little Bible study group is illegal, and wouldn't believe you if you told them.

... OR COMING IN

A more recent trend is for 'unregistered' churches to register with the authorities but keep their denominational distinctives and not be part of the TSPM. This legal fudge has served some older indigenous denominations like Watchman Nee's Little Flock Assemblies for a number of years. Nowadays it is an expanding category: total churches and meeting points registered with the government, TSPM or not, exceeds 50,000.[38]

This trend of semi-registration could be understood as any or all of these:

- a quiet admission by the authorities that the TSPM will never embrace all of Chinese Christianity
- another expression of the Chinese Communist determination to register, monitor and control everything
- a straw in the wind that in the future, Chinese government regulation of the Christian movement may be wide and shallow, rather than deep and narrow.

It isn't clear at the moment, and deciding whether or not to register is tricky. It can mean that your church is 'fulfilling all righteousness' and becoming legal. It can also mean better access to Bibles and Christian books and a certain freedom from persecution.

But not necessarily. In Wenzhou, churches that had been previously persecuted were left quite alone after registering, until autumn 2000 when the authorities suddenly destroyed 200 registered churches and put pastors under close surveillance. Western mission agency Open Doors quoted one pastor from Wenzhou,

'We came up to the surface in all good faith, but all the gains have been wiped out and now we are sitting ducks.'[39]

LIFE ON THE UNDERGROUND

In February 2002, a New-York-based political activist named Li Shi-xiong unveiled an archive of papers three metres high, which contained 5,000 detailed testimonies of people arrested, and sometimes tortured and jailed by the authorities. His archive also included 17,000 less-complete testimonies of arrest, and records of 117 deaths in custody and of more than 500 people sent to labour camps. All were of 'religious' people, many of them, Christians.

The head of China's Religious Affairs Bureau, Ye Xiaowen, toured the United States in 2001 and proclaimed that the government had initiated a 'golden time' for religions in China. Around the same time, the then-president of China, Jiang Zemin said to an American congressional audience, 'I am looking forward to seeing a church on one side of every village and a mosque on the other side.'[40]

In reality, China's leaders are happy to treat any expression of Christianity outside the registered church as if it were a cult—and they like to 'infiltrate' and 'smash' cults.

China's treatment of the South China Church is a case in point. For much of 2001, Chinese authorities were targeting this large, unregistered Protestant group. Offices were raided. Many peo-ple were arrested. At one point several of the leaders were sentenced to death.

Lawyers, who were not Christians, were appointed to handle the appeal and were shocked when they met the prisoners and found that all had been severely tortured. They saw shackles that had cut so deeply for so long that skin was growing over them.

International outcry (and the then-imminent visit of President Bush), seemed to produce an unexpected result to the appeal. The death sentences were dropped, as were the 'evil cult' charges. Some of the leaders were declared innocent and released, others were put on sentences that could mean a quiet release later. One was still sentenced to 15 years' prison.

Once media attention shifted, persecution quietly resumed.

The South China Church is not really an exception. You don't have to look too far (especially away from the coastal cities) to find pastors who always take an overnight bag with them to church meetings, in case they have to spend the night in prison; or communion and baptisms happening out in the woods, sometimes at night, to keep out of the way of the authorities; or church meetings raided, property impounded, fines raised, buildings destroyed.

– 5 –
Issues for the Church: Internal

TO DO

Let's examine the Chinese Church's 'to do' list. If anything is calculated to drive us to prayer on behalf of our Christian brothers and sisters, surely it's this—on top of the harrassment, the persecution, the shortages, the struggles to live and thrive in China, there are battles to fight on many fronts.

Mention of these challenges needs to be set against the wonderful achievements of the Chinese Church. Outside observers get a certain sense of being unfit to tie the sandals of these Christians: Where else have so many millions turned to Christ, in such a short time, as in China? Where else have Christians paid such a price in blood and tears as China's Christians? But it would be tragic for all these gains to be squandered.

Let's vaguely divide the list into internal and external challenges: by internal we mean problems among people who are already within the Church; by external we mean looking at the Church's unpaid debts to those outside.

ONE SHORTAGE—MANY PROBLEMS

The Chinese Church, both in its official and unofficial parts, has a core of mature Christians, female and male, proven faithful through many trials, with a deep Biblical knowledge, wise, and capable of providing leadership and stability throughout the Church. Some are intellectuals, some peasants, all are godly: they would adorn any congregation.

The problem is, there aren't nearly enough of them—not enough to stop village congregations 'being blown here and there by every wind of teaching',[41] not enough to stop 'savage wolves'[42] from stealing the flock, not enough to offer a grand vision for building a nation on Christian principles.

Many problems stem from this basic shortage. Here are some, in no particular order:

1. Workaholism

The toll on leaders and their families is high, especially in the unregistered sector. Family relationships and mental health can take a battering under the pressures to care for rapidly expanding congregations. A former leader of a house-church network known as Brother Yun has written, 'Not surprisingly, many of the marriages and families of the leaders from [one particular house church network] are in complete disarray. Many appear to be "successful" in their ministries while their families are falling apart. For all the strengths possessed by China's house-churches, this area is one of its weakest points.'[43]

2. Accountability

A piece for the official Christian magazine, *Tian Feng*, outlined a number of 'holes to be mended in the fishing net' of the Chinese Church. It pointed out that, 'some unfortunate situations do exist, where people of little commitment and with unclear motivations join the ranks of church workers. [This is especially true in the TSPM and is a thinly-veiled criticism of the Party habit of foisting its own people on TSPM congregations.] There are also those who, after entering the church, become distracted and change, maybe even become criminal. The church lacks an effective system of control.'[44] Also, 'many meeting points do not have a proper management structure, or finances are controlled by single individuals.'

If these are problems in the TSPM/CCC, they must also be dangers for the unregistered churches, as must be the challenge of funds from abroad, often given both with great enthusiasm and woeful lack of discernment.

3. Cults

If we defined cult by Western standards we would mean groups that either (a) denied the doctrine of the Trinity in some way and/or (b) made something other than faith in Christ as the central issue in the gospel. Often this 'something other' is 'someone other', a charismatic leader without whose blessing you can't be really saved.

EASTERN LIGHTNING

The Eastern Lightning cult is led by a woman who thinks the text in Matthew 24:27—'for as lightning that comes from the east is visible even in the west'—refers to her and that she is the Messiah for a new age. It is unusual in that it specifically targets the unregistered church.

Its members will go along to church meetings, become known, then ask leaders to visit them to give some help or counsel. The leaders are then kidnapped and brainwashed—surrounded constantly by people who are all teaching the Eastern Lightning version of truth. Visions and deliverances are play-acted, and sexual favours forced on the leaders. Eastern Lightning has also been working among Chinese churches overseas.

In April 2002, Eastern Lightning kidnapped the entire top leadership of one of China's largest housegroup networks, China Gospel Fellowship. It took a little while for people to realize what had happened, because everyone thought this was just a standard round-up by the Public Security Bureau. The CGF leaders were eventually freed, however, though all took time to recover from the experience.[45]

Tony Lambert estimates that by the Western definition perhaps 5% to 10% of the unregistered Christian community are cults. Almost all are some form of peasant messianic movement. Many are only local or regional in scope.[46]

However cults are a serious problem for the Church. For these reasons:

- *Some become nationally significant and a direct threat to the Christian movement*—such as the Shouters in the 1980s, the cult of the

'Established King' in the 1990s, or Eastern Lightning in the first decade of the new millennium. Eastern Lightning is perhaps the worst because it single-mindedly targets existing Christian groups (see box).

- *They give an excuse for attacks on all unregistered Christians.* Party officials are not good at discriminating between cults and orthodox, unregistered churches. In a major Party review of religious policy, the then-Premier Zhu Rongji insisted 'efforts should be made to fight against any illegal religions'.[47] As long as the curious idea of 'illegal religions' persists, local officials can declare open season on unregistered churches. There have been cases when Christians have been arrested for owning 'subversive materials' and it turned out that the 'subversive materials' (a copy of the Bible and a hymnbook) were books legally published by the TSPM.

4. Ghettoism

The criticism could be made that the unofficial Christian community (especially) shows signs of behaving like an obscure mystery religion rather than 'the city of God.'

The core symptom is a dangerous reluctance to engage with the real world. Many would make belief in a Saturday Sabbath or some pre-millennial eschatological scheme a central article of faith. Many Christians have had an encounter with Jesus as the great healer but have not gone on to work out what the Christian faith really means in ordinary life.

A Western journalist exploring Henan province gave a ride to an old farmer and asked him, 'Do you believe in Buddhism around here?' 'Oh no, not here,' the farmer replied. 'Here we all follow the Lord!' The farmer then gave the journalist false directions so that instead of being taken to visit a tomb, as promised, the journalist ended up dropping the farmer off at his own house.[48]

Sometimes, there is a bit of denial of real problems lest the gospel 'looks bad'. This reflects the Chinese cultural instinct to keep all problems within the family. But as we know from painful experience in the West, with our history of fraudulent preachers, hypocrisy of this kind (we have to call it that) can wreak havoc for future generations of Christian witness.

A frequent visitor to the Chinese Church told a true story about a brave old woman whom he knew well.[49] During the Cultural Revolution, some Red Guards had beaten her every day. This had gone on for ten years. Yet her testimony was all of how she was kept in peace, was full of joy, and was overflowing with compassion for the Red Guards.

'But did you have any doubts that God was with you?' I would press her.' Did you ever feel discouraged?' And her reply was always the same,

'Never!'

But then, on what was probably his 15th visit, he questioned her more closely. At first she insisted, that every moment was 'sheer joy.' He reminded her that no-one else was listening. They were old friends. She could be honest. Finally he got a fresh story:

She paused and then said in a shocked whisper, 'No, I have to say it was awful, but I can't say too loudly.'

She then described how, through many very dark times, including when she was almost suicidal, God did indeed gently sustain and encourage her. It wasn't 'pure joy', but it was sustaining grace.

He concluded, 'I think it is a fact that many persecuted Christians self-censor their spiritual struggles ... we should pray that they might feel able to share these struggles more honestly.' Let us hope this same self-censorship doesn't apply when big moral issues (like money, power, and sex) have to be faced.

5. *Theological reconstruction*

The 'theological reconstruction' project comes from the top leadership of the TSPM. The starting point was the 1998 book by the long-time leader of the TSPM, Bishop K H Ting, called *Love Never Ends* in English translation.[50] In it, Ting states his belief that 'socialism is love on a grand scale, organized love, love which has taken shape as a social system.' To make China's Church serve its nation properly, he wants the importance of loving acts to be seen as the central theme of the Christian faith. He also wants to de-emphasize the idea of 'justification by faith alone, through grace alone' as the essential core.

Ting's project has been strenuously opposed by Evangelicals both within and outside China, including theological teachers at the heart of the TSPM/CCC. All of them see it as a campaign to take an axe to the Church's Biblical roots and make Chinese Christianity as dried-up and fruitless as liberal Christianity in the West.[51]

The theological construction China actually needs—these critics would argue—starts with a fresh, deep, Chinese encounter with the scriptures.

CONCLUSION

All of this highlights the core need for the Chinese Church: more and more people who in the apostle John's phrase, 'walk in truth'.

– 6 –
Issues for the Church: External

Now a look at the challenges outside the Church.

1. THE MAJORITY

Even in a Church full of evangelists, as China's is, evangelizing the majority is the pressing need.

To most of us—who live in contexts that are not China-sized—China's Church looks big, one of the great new facts of the world. But a community of even 70m or 90m people is not really big at all in a country of 1.3bn. Nor is the move to Christianity the only trend, or even the major national trend: a reviving Buddhism has more adherents than the Church. Individual sects like Falun Gong and Qigong claim similar-sized followings to the whole Christian movement. Many other religious groups are busy in China—Mormons, Bahai, followers of Japanese sects or Indian gurus like Sai Baba. And materialism may take the edge from people's appetite, dulling their desire to change.

Yet now is a special time of enormous responsiveness, never before seen in China, maybe never to be seen to the same extent again. The urgency and primacy of evangelism can hardly be overstressed.

One long-time worker in China told us, 'the fruit is not only ripe for harvest but some of it is falling to the ground to be taken away by other philosophies and religions.'[52]

Another suggested that if gospel preaching has typically a 3% response in the West, it has more like a 50-60% response in some parts of China.[53]

It seems unlikely to me that this response rate and subsequent rapid church growth will continue for very long. China's fellow heavyweight on the world stage, India, saw spectacular church growth for about 70 years, say between 1870 and 1940, but the Christian community there has been stuck at below 3% of the population ever since. There has been faithful evangelism throughout India, but a great season of responsiveness passed with the harvest only just beginning to be gathered. Let us pray this is not repeated in China.

So the Chinese Church's greatest challenge is to make the very most of this extraordinary season and make disciples among the 1.2 billion Han Chinese.

Among the least-reached of the Han are the Party members (say 60m), the armed forces (nearly 3m), and the 'lost generation' who were in their late teens or twenties during the mad years of the Cultural Revolution.

Then, China's provinces have seen vastly different responses to the gospel, mostly depending on the success of Protestant missionary work in the hundred years up to 1949. The most Christian provinces are towards China's east and south-east, plus Yunnan in the south-west. The far south, the north, many central and western provinces are much less Christian—see the map at the back of the book.

2. THE CHILDREN

Ministry among China's 360m under-18s is a further great need. The Chinese State is still determined to orientate all its children into 'Marxist-Leninist-Mao-Zedong' thought, even though few believe in it, and then to recruit them into its own youth organizations. The law bans all evangelism of under-18s, even of children of registered Christians.

People who are brave and visionary enough to risk running a Sunday School endure a woeful lack of material. The law prevents even the official church from producing teaching materials. Some overseas Christian groups do produce books or courses and children's Bibles. Some groups run clandestine Sunday School teacher training. But overall, as Tony Lambert points out, 'the lack of Sunday School work and children's ministry constitutes a serious weakness in what is otherwise a flourishing scene.'[54] Ross Paterson, who coordinates a ministry supporting the Chinese Church, reports a brisk demand for his organisation's Sunday School materials, called 'Love-18'.[55]

3. THE MINORITIES

China has, officially, 55 minority peoples. Rather like H J Heinz's '57 Varieties', China's 55 minorities are a convenient fiction made venerable by long use, not by any inherent relation to the facts.

The current best count of China's minorities, patiently compiled in Paul Hattaway's *Operation China*, is perhaps 490 different groups, encompassing in all about 100m people. The number of groups is likely to increase still more. Yunnan (itself home to over 250 of these groups) is just one area that needs to be more effectively studied.

China's minorities have vastly different stories to tell. Some of the bigger groups (Tibetans and Uyghurs for example) have known severe suffering because China has suppressed their independence movements and persecuted their religious faith. In Xinjiang Uyghur Autonomous Region (where the Uyghurs live, on the fringes of the Taklamakan desert) and the Tibet—Xizang Tibetan Autonomous Region (the Tibetan plateau), killings on the scale of Tiananmen Square have taken place, but mostly outside the scrutiny of western journalists.

China's minorities are poor by global standards. However, Chinese rule has brought benefits, perhaps especially for the smaller peoples. China's leaders seem genuinely concerned to fight for a better life for the minority peoples. Minorities get some privileges—a seat for a representative in the People's Congress, for example, and fewer restrictions on family planning.

Interestingly, some Christian-based NGOs have found a fruitful ministry among minority communities in partnership with local government. Christian groups have built bridges, dug wells, provided cisterns, developed appropriate technology, worked in orphanages, created micro-credit schemes, planted trees, built technical colleges, and much else, in excellent demonstrations of holistic Christian care.

More than 350 of the minority groups are less than 1% Christian and more than 250 have no known Christians among them. Most have no Christian teaching material in their own language.[56]

China may be realistically 4-7% Christian according to the best estimates,[57] so the minorities still stand out also as significantly deprived of Christian witness, and are a major challenge for both the Chinese and overseas Church.

4. THE POOR AND NEEDY

The challenge of China's poor and needy makes you admire any government heroic enough to even try to tackle the problems. A sample:

• Old, smokestack industries and rural enterprises going bust, making people redundant and thus removing whole families, whole towns, from the old communal shelter that offered jobs and homes, and free schools and clinics.

- Farmers struggling to make ends meet. Many are leaving the land and forming a large underclass of perhaps 100m-200m migrant workers. These people will work in the cities in rotten working conditions, for poor pay, seven days a week.

- Old people with little pension and only one grandchild, shared between four of them, to provide for their old age.

- Unwanted children. China's one-child policy can lead to the rejection of children who don't come up to scratch, through physical or mental handicap or simply through being born female.

- Disabled people: China has, for example, 13m blind people.

The Chinese government's main strategy in the face of this catalogue of need is to keep pumping away at growing the economy, sacrificing much of the old welfare provision on the way. That leaves many open wounds in society which the Church could help heal.

Christians are stepping in, often informally or in low-key ways, but also with increasing visibility. In late 2002, the TSPM/CCC established a Social Service Department to give national coordination and prominence to Christian social action. They initially counted 45 projects in various regions, 'mostly homes for the elderly, kindergartens and clinics, but also rehabilitation for handicapped children and support for the school-less.[58]

5. BEING PROPHETIC

The Church is steward not only of the good news about God's forgiveness, but also of being 'salt and light'—shedding light in dark corners, and changing the whole flavour of the nation. 'Let justice roll on like a river, righteousness like a never-failing stream!'[59] Part of Christian worship is helping to overhaul and renew the way the nation works for everyone's good. In China, this role still belongs to the Party: it claims the prophetic right to guide Church and nation in paths of righteousness.

Outside observers will note that the unregistered church is not quick to go public with criticism of the Chinese state, and the Three-Self churches are little better, though a few leaders have occasionally put their names to calls for greater democracy, for example. Great injustices, it seems, occur without a murmur from the Church.

As ever, in China, however, things may not be all they seem. As we have seen, it is most uncultural to publicly criticize leaders. A far wiser strategy in the Chinese context may be quietly to get on with 'doing righteousness', encourage the good in officials rather than criticizing the bad, save face, show respect, maintain harmony, and let Christian lifestyles do the talking.

6. 'BACK TO JERUSALEM'

In 1949, at the very end of the traditional missionary era, Phyllis Thompson of the China Inland Mission wrote a letter home:

> The thing that has impressed me most has been the strange, unaccountable urge of a number of different Chinese groups of Christians to press forward in faith, taking the gospel towards the West. I know of at least five different groups ... It seems like a movement of the Spirit which is irresistible. The striking thing is that they are disconnected, and in most cases seem to know nothing about each other. Yet all are convinced that the Lord is sending them to the western borders to preach the gospel.[60]

People felt that God was putting a call on the Chinese Church to preach the gospel from China all the way 'back to Jerusalem', starting churches everywhere as they went.

Through the past 2000 years, these Christians argued, the gospel had mostly travelled west and south, to the Mediterranean region, Europe, Africa, the Americas, and then the Pacific Rim and China. Now, God was calling Chinese churches to help shoulder the burden of completing the circle and bringing the gospel to the Buddhist, Hindu, Muslim and Jewish homelands.

This movement was quickly stopped after the birth of the New China in 1949. But the vision didn't die.

In 1995, Brother Yun was preaching about this vision when an old man in one congregation, deeply moved, asked to speak. He identified himself as one of the small band who had walked all the way to Kashgar near the Soviet border in 1948, pursuing a 'back to Jerusalem' vision.[61] At that point the Communists had taken control and the man, whose name was Simon Zhao, had spent the forty years in prison. His testimony, related by Brother Yun, was this:

'Every evening, for forty years in the labour camp, I faced towards the west, in the direction of Jerusalem, and cried out to the Lord "Oh God, I'll never be able to reach Jerusalem on foot. Our vision has perished. Heavenly Father, I pray that you will raise up a new generation of Christians in China who are willing to lay down their lives to take the gospel all the way back to where it started in Jerusalem."'

In 1996 Chinese house-church networks began to recommit themselves to this vision. They have now, in the early years of the new millennium, begun to send workers to many of the minority peoples, spurred on in part by *Operation China*. And six leaders representing some of the major house-church networks have pledged to mobilise 100,000 missionaries from China to take the gospel 'back to Jerusalem.' (The current total of Protestant missionaries in the world, sent from one country to minister in another, is around 98,000.)[62]

And they are serious. People are being trained in bush mission schools. Some have already gone to different countries by various means, perhaps by starting a Chinese restaurant. Some are training specially to reach Muslims or Buddhists.

Chinese house-church Christians bring to the missions enterprise courage, faith, expectancy and boldness, and a willingness to suffer and lay down their lives. They come, as it were, already spiritual battle-hardened veterans, though now facing cultural contexts and logistical problems that are vastly different from those at home.

The numbers so far involved are hundreds, not thousands, and these pioneers are tasting all the great problems of missionary work. Some end up spending all their time ministering among the Chinese. Visa problems have claimed others. Some, working among Tibetan Buddhist communities for example, have found a complete lack of response—a very unusual experience for a Chinese Christian, hard to explain to supporters back home.

The movement is also endangered by the enthusiasm of Western Christians, who, hearing about it, are perhaps too ready to give money without enquiring whether money is really needed, or will be spent well, or will be devoted to the Back to Jerusalem vision at all.

And at the moment the 'Back to Jerusalem' vision doesn't have too many concrete instances of success to draw upon—or, for that matter, too many examples of failure to learn from. The experiences of older mission-sending countries (like Brazil or South Korea, say, which themselves enjoyed a first great blossoming of mission growth around 20 years ago) could prove hugely valuable.

Most likely the story of missions from China will follow much the same wandering path as missions *to* China, or anywhere else, did: great vision, great disappointment, great fruit. Depending on your point of view it is easy to praise the BTJ movement to the skies or feel anxious over its failings. But the big story is that the Chinese house-churches are being gripped by a mission vision, a new chapter in missions is being written, and it will make the world a different place.

– 7 –
Partnership in the gospel

How can we express partnership in the gospel with this amazing Church in this extraordinary land? We only have room to outline some general ideas here.

start with a reminder from Tony Lambert (I added the emphasis):

The revival of the last three decades has been a work of God through a totally indigenous movement. The missionaries had been expelled by 1952. Radio and literature work had significant impact beginning in the late 70s, but otherwise, until recently, Western input and impact was minimal. We must face the fact that God, through His suffering people, raised up to Himself a glorious church without our programmes, money or involvement, but not apart from our prayers.[63]

Paul Hattaway, talking about the involvement of overseas Christians with the Chinese Church, borrows from the Biblical story of Elijah and the widow of Zarephath.[64] The overseas Church, claims Hattaway, often seems to think it is like Elijah, helping out the poor struggling widow of the Chinese Church.

He insists it's the other way around. The Chinese Church is the prophetic, spiritually powerful figure, while churches overseas are more like the widow—impoverished, but helping out a little materially.

My own observations are almost the opposite to his: the Western churches that I am involved in are almost desperate to associate with Chinese Christianity precisely because it seems so spiritually alive, with its *Acts*-like whiff of revival, miracles, and jailbreaks. We want everything that can somehow link us with Chinese Christianity, its bold faith, its magnificent courage in adversity, its numerical success. That can lead to almost uncritical admiration for all Christian things unregistered and Chinese, and that helps no-one.

Further, the gods of the West—money, status, and technology, which we love to get others to worship—are not the answer. The Chinese Church, both official and unofficial, is just as capable of being corrupted by these as (say) American Christian TV has been. Injudicious giving from overseas could be a great tragedy for the Chinese Church. Having faced down brutal enemies, it could end up being blessed to death by its friends.

So some humility is in order. Ross Paterson, from his long experience at the interface between overseas and Chinese Christianity, offers a cool perspective:

> *The Chinese Church comprises ordinary people, just like you and me, with failings and weaknesses. It is these people we are serving. We must serve them with long-term commitment, focusing on the long-term product.*[65]

PARTNERSHIP FROM OVERSEAS

The general areas in which overseas Christians can bring a love-offering to Chinese Christianity can be easily listed:

1. *Prayer:* This is the strategy that appears to have served the cause of Christianity in China best of all.

2. *Person to person:* Personal contacts (either by living in China for a while or looking out for Chinese visitors in our country) is in many ways the most natural, obvious, and fruitful way of working—opening one's eyes to the wonderful Chinese world, and perhaps at some level strengthening the Christian movement among the Chinese.

3. *Resources*: Everyone involved with the Chinese Church is concerned about it being built up, strengthened, attaining 'to the whole measure of the fullness of Christ.'[66] Overseas Christians surely can play a part here, but need great wisdom not to lead the Chinese Church into an unhealthy dependence on outsiders, to force on them our denominational distinctives, or to give money without proper accounting as to where the money is going.

4. *The NGO route:* China has a stated goal of 'small state; large society' which has opened the route for NGOs local and foreign to serve in China. This has already led to much excellent work: cisterns dug, health clinics built, vocational training provided for the handicapped, orphanages revolutionized—and this is only the beginning.

THE LAW AND GRACE

We don't travel very far down this road, however, before the large issue of Christian work and Chinese law looms up.

It is easy to break the law in China. Since Christians place a high value on not just being law-abiding but actually law-upholding, this is a problem. Here is section 17 of the applicable rules for overseas workers:

Aliens may not engage in the following missionary activities within Chinese territory

• Appointing religious personnel among Chinese citizens

• Developing religious followers among Chinese citizens;

• Preaching and expounding the scripture at the sites for religious activities [ie TSPM churches and meeting points] without permission;

• Preaching and expounding the scripture or conducting religious gathering activities at places outside the lawfully registered sites for religious activities;

• Producing or selling religious books, journals, religious audio-visual products, religious electronic goods or other religious articles;

• Distributing religious propaganda materials;

• Other missionary activities.[67]

People working with NGOs also struggle with working in a situation where laws are 'so vague, contradictory or burdensome that they end up being circumvented or ignored'.[68]

Everyone actively involved in serving China by something other than prayer has to face the fact that they could end up in trouble with the law. What should they do? The advice seems to be: don't be paralysed by it, don't glory in it, and remember you're a Christian. Ross Paterson again:

> I would warn the church against two extremes: on the one hand focusing on just the miracles and the exciting things, or on the other hand being so afraid of arrest (whether of ourselves or others) that we don't dare do anything at all. We must serve the church there soberly and wisely.[69]

In China, law is in the hands of local officials, rather than officials being in the hands of the law. (In Mandarin this is called *rénzhì*, rule by individuals, rather than *fǎzhì*, the rule of law.)[70] Laws are made broad and ambiguous—setting direction, but leaving all the discretion with the local officials. You can appeal to a higher official, but you are unlikely to succeed, since it will make the higher official look bad (he or she supervises the lower official, and you are questioning their judgment).

Almost everything attributed to the 'government', and certainly every act of persecution or obstruction to Christian work, actually comes down to the decision of an official somewhere.

But here is the opportunity for Christian service. Officials are themselves victims of the system. Every local official is subject to arbitrary decisions from officials above; each one is a cog in a Party machine that works largely by fear and distrust, and often doesn't work at all, being subverted by corruption.

The Christian course in such a culture is to live lovingly, humbly, sincerely, with personal integrity, and with particular scrupulousness about maintaining the best possible honest relationships with officials. And blessing them with prayers and good attitudes. The chaotic legal system in China is actually a golden opportunity for Christians to subvert a corrupt system with honourable acts, to overcome evil with good. Chinese Christians often understand this instinctively: outsiders, much less so.

The great sin that overseas Christians must guard against is that of cultural arrogance, not giving proper respect to the authorities and to the culture.

Giving this proper respect will not guarantee a lack of persecution or trouble. But it will ensure a clear conscience and also ensure that whether there is trouble or not, the kingdom of God moves forward, not backward.

The apostle Peter's advice seems particularly appropriate as a guide for ministry in China: 'Live such good lives ... that, though they may accuse you of doing wrong, they may see your good deeds and glorify God.'[71]

SOME PRINCIPLES

It is complex and perhaps unwise to delve further into all the different ways the overseas Church is seeking to be partners in the gospel with the Chinese Church. Some ways are open and public, others deliberately quiet and low-key.

But some general principles of work seem clear. We should prefer work that is quiet rather than sensational; honouring to the Chinese State— even in its current Communist dynasty—rather than running it down; concerned with building up the Chinese Church rather than exploiting it for cheap publicity; willing to be arrested for the gospel but unwilling to be disrespectful to the authorities; in a loving partnership with Chinese Christians but aware of our failings and of theirs.

THE ROLE OF OUTSIDERS

I once heard a Chinese pastor discussing the role of foreign Christians in the growth of Christ's Kingdom in China ... When asked what purpose foreigners could best serve, he responded simply, 'Foreigners are able to go to places where we Chinese Christians rarely go. They can talk to people we rarely meet. Foreign Christians are like the spade that breaks up the soil.' Afterwards, we need to step aside so that the Chinese labourers can come in and plant seeds, water the seedlings, and eventually harvest the crop.[72]

NOTES

CHAPTER 1

1 'By the end of 1999, the population under the poverty line in the rural areas had decreased from over 250 million in the late 1970s to 34 million, down from 33% to around 3% of the total rural population.' White Paper on Population in China, published by the China Population and Information Research Centre (see www.cpirc.org.cn/whitepaper.htm).

2 He was in effective charge for several years before 1997.

3 World Bank figures; see for example www.worldbank.org/html/schools/regions/eap/china.htm

4 See for example, the *Economist*, July 22nd 2000.

5 Human Rights Watch *World Report 2003*, available on hrw.org

6 I am very indebted to the helpful booklet *An Introduction to the Mainland Chinese Soul*, available from LEAD Consulting, PO Box 32026, Raleigh, NC 27622 USA.

7 I'm indebted to Sheryl Wudunn for that insight. See Nicholas D Kirstoff and Sheryl Wudunn in *China Wakes* (London: Nicholas Brealey Publishing 1998), p 56.

8 For example, Geremie Barme, an Australian scholar, talks of peasants' fascination with the miraculous (in this context, with Qigong miracle workers, but the same would apply to Christian miracle workers), 'It's a classic end-of-dynasty phenomenon ... you always get this kind of wierd stuff when the dynasty is collapsing.' (Quoted by *New York Times* journalists Nicholas D Kirstoff and Sheryl Wudunn in *China Wakes*, p 133.

9 *Village of Despair*, Sunday *Times* Magazine (London) March 9th 2003.

10 This story was uncovered by New York *Times* reporter Sheryl Wudun, and documented in Nicholas D Kristof and Sheryl Wudunn *China Wakes*, pp 94-101.

11 Press reports, June 25 2003.

CHAPTER 2

12 See my book *Briefings: The Silk Road* (Carlisle, UK: Paternoster Press 2001), pp 9-10.

13 *East Asia's Billions* (the magazine of OMF International UK), January 2000, p 6.

14 John Foster *Five Minutes a Saint*, (London 1963: SCM press), p 95.

15 See Stephen Neill, *A History of Christian Missions*, (London: Penguin Books 1964).

16 R G Tiedemann, *China and its Neighbours*, in A Hastings, ed, *A World History of Christianity* (London 1999: Cassells), p 372.

17 Some argue that Catholic testimony actually lasted from the Franciscan missions under the Yuan. Tiedemann in A Hastings, ed, *A World History of Christianity*, p 376 cites Bernward H Willeke OFM, 'Did Catholicism in the Yuan Dynasty survive until the present?' *Tripod* 47 (October 1988), pp 64-9

18 Kenneth Scott Latourette *A History of Christianity*, Vol II, (New York: Harper & Row 1975), p 941.

19 He based his work on the gospels on Jesuit translation that had been

found in the British Library and that he worked on before he left for China.
0 See the account of Morrison's life in Peter Hammond, *The Greatest Century of Missions* (Cape Town: Christian Liberty Books 2002), pp 78-81.

CHAPTER 3

1 Ezekiel 37: 1-15.
2 Tony Lambert described a trip to Yongjia County in Greater Wenzhou Municipality: 'Over the next four hours driving through the region I must have seen more than a dozen churches, and doubtless missed as many more, in every village and hamlet we passed through ... Just as remarkable was the open Christian witness of many of the inhabitants ... Yongjia County with a total population of 730,000 has a registered evangelical Christian (adult) population of 130,000 souls.' (*China's Christian Millions* (UK: OMF, 1999), p 19.)
3 Theresa Carino, *30 million bibles printed in China*, Amity News Service, Jan/Feb 2003 (www.amityfoundation.org/ANS/Articles/ans2003/ans2003.2/2003_2_9.htm).
4 Bibles are not yet available on the open market in China—you can only get them through Church sources (either legal or illegal)—so it is a fair assumption that most Bibles go to people who have some significant commitment to the Christian faith.
5 Interview, June 2002.
6 *UBS World Report* 354, October 2000, p 25.
7 Johnstone, P and Mandryk, J, *Operation World* (UK: Paternoster Press, 2001), p 160-161.
8 The official total for baptised adult church members in 1949 is 700,000; mission researchers put this figure at 1m. The higher figure given here for the Protestant community is an attempt to include children of believers, and not-yet-baptized adherents.

CHAPTER 4

29 *New China News Agency*, 21 September 2000.
30 Tony Lambert *China's Christian Millions*, p 30.
31 See *7 Years of Prayer for China*, Bulletin 5, Spring 2003, p 2, published by Open Doors (www.opendoor-suk.org).
32 Wang Rongwei, *One Black Sheep that Harmed the Whole Flock*. English translation of *Tian Feng* article, Amity News Service, July/August 2002. (www.amityfoundation.org)
33 *Chinese Government Reassesses Religion*, Amity News Service, Jan/Feb 2002. Jiang said, 'Religion cannot be extinguished through administrative measures'. ... Instead, he said, the aim is to promote 'the adaptation of religion and socialist society to each other.'
34 In March/April 2003, Amity News Service profiled 'Bamboo Church' in Xiamen, Fujian Province. In its former life, this TSPM church was planted by missionaries from the Reformed Church of America. This thriving church (2,500 in the congregation) was entirely open about having a youth fellowship and a 300-strong Sunday School, staffed by 40 volunteers. See Don Snow, *Reformed Roots, Post-Denominational Shoots*, Amity News Service, March/April 2003, www.amityfoundation.org. A success-

ful youth group was profiled by the Amity News Service in May/June 2001.

35 Tony Lambert *China's Christian Millions*, p 31.

36 The nation of Brazil offers an interesting comparison. Observers will tell you confidently that there has been huge church growth in Brazil. But even in that nation, giving accurate statistical expression is hard. In 1993, *Operation World* published a figure of 14 million people affiliated with the Assemblies of God—reflecting the best data available. In 2001, with better data, the equivalent figure was 4 million.

37 From an interview with Paul Hattaway, Thailand, August 2002. The figure came from six major house church networks pooling their individual figures.

38 According to a press release from the news agency Compass Direct, *Christians Confront Religious Bureaucracy*, 14/04/03.

39 Open Doors, *7 Years of Prayer for China*, Bulletin 5, Spring 2003, p 1.

40 See *Christianity Today*, March 11th 2002 Vol. 46, No. 3, Page 38 (www.christianitytoday.com).

CHAPTER 5

41 Ephesians 4:14.

42 Acts 20:29.

43 Brother Yun with Paul Hattaway *The Heavenly Man* (UK 2002: Monarch), p 225.

44 Fan Aishi, *Mending the Church's Fishing Net* Tian Feng, Feb 2003; see www.amityfoundation.org

45 You can read their account on www.chinaforjesus.com

46 Tony Lambert bases his analysis on internal government document that compared the numbers of meeting places of 'orthodox' house-church Christians, TSPM members, and cults in the province of Henan.

47 *Chinese Government Reassesses Religion*, Amity News Service, Jan/Feb 2002 (www.amityfoundation.org).

48 John Gittings, *Real China*, (London 1998: Simon and Schuster), p 61.

49 Alex Buchan, *Quotes to Live By*, booklet produced by Open Doors Canada, 2001, pp 28-29.

50 K H Ting, *Love Never Ends* (Nanjing 1998: Amity Printing Co Ltd).

51 For a sample of the criticism see, for example, Dr Werner Burklin, *The Role of Theological Education for a Changing Church and Society in China* (see http://www.bucer.de/theology-consultation/Docs/China.pdf). Essentially the 'theological reconstruction' project appears to be supplanting 'justification by faith' with 'justification by love', on which ticket (to put it crudely) Communist Party heroes who deny the gospel can nevertheless go to heaven.

CHAPTER 6

52 Personal communication.

53 Interview with Paul Hattaway, August 2002.

54 Tony Lambert, *China's Christian Millions—the costly revival*, p 136.

55 Interviewed November 30 and December 1 2002.

56 One or two minorities—such as the Lisu in the south-west—are officially listed as Christian by the Chinese government, because they are at least 50% Christian.

7 *Operation World* gives an estimate for 2000 of a total Christian community of 7.25%, 92m people (adults and children).

8 Wang Rongwei *Living Out Christian Service Through Love to One's Neighbour*, Amity News Service, Jan/Feb 2003. (www.amityfoundation.org)

9 Amos 5:24 (NIV).

0 Tony Lambert unearthed this gem, and he discusses the Back to Jerusalem movement with his customary judiciousness in the *China Insight Newsletters* of November/December 2002 and March/April 2003, published on www.omf.org

1 Brother Yun with Paul Hattaway *The Heavenly Man* (UK 2002: Monarch), p 280-284.

2 Patrick Johnstone and Jason Mandryk, *Operation World*, p 4.

CHAPTER 7

3 Tony Lambert, *The Changing Face of China's Church* in ChinaSource, 1999. (See http://www.chsource.org/ChangingChina.htm)

64 Personal interview, August 2002. The story of Elijah and the widow of Zarephath is in 1 Kings 17: 7-24.

65 Ross Paterson, personal interview, November 2002.

66 Ephesians 4:13.

67 *Regulations for Management of the Religious Activities of Foreigners within the PRC*, published in English translation in *China Daily* on September 27, 2000.

68 Carol Hamrin, *China's Society Makes a Comeback*, ChinaSource, Fall 2002 (Vol 4, No.3), p 4.

69 Ross Paterson.

70 Nicholas D Kirstoff and Sheryl Wudunn in *China Wakes*, p 96.

71 I Peter 2:12.

72 Andrew Kaiser in *Work and Ministry, Foreign Nonprofit Organizations and the Church in China*, in ChinaSource, Fall 2002, Vol 4, No. 3, p 10.

BIBLIOGRAPHY

... of a handful of some of the very best books

An Introduction to the Mainland Chinese Soul, (2001) available from LEAD Consulting, PO Box 32026, Raleigh, NC 27622 USA.

A very helpful entrée to cultural issues.

Hattaway, Paul
2001 *Operation China* (Carlisle, UK: Piquant).

Unique, outstanding, comprehensive resource that defines and describes China's 490 people groups and their response to the gospel.

2003 *Back to Jerusalem* (Carlisle, UK: Piquant).

Story of the 'Back to Jerusalem' movement.

Jung Chang
1991 *Wild Swans* (London: Harper Collins).

Inside view of China's 20th century told through a family history. A classic.

Lambert, Tony
1994 *The Resurrection of the Chinese Church* (USA: OMF/Harold Shaw).

Carefully compiled, detailed, authoritative account from one of the mission world's best-equipped scholars of Chinese Church developments.

1999 *China's Christian Millions: The costly revival* (UK:OMF/Monarch).

'The fruit of three decades of research, reflection and writing.'

Mackay, Belinda
2001 *China Dancer: Cameos of Life in China* (UK: Gabriel Resources).

First-hand account of an expatriate in China and a good introduction to issues for people planning to work in China.

Moffett, Samuel
1992 *A History of Christianity in Asia* (New York).

The standard, superb, source.

Paterson, Ross
2000 *The Continuing Heartcry for China* (UK: Sovereign World).

Yamamori & Chan
2002 *Witnesses To Power—Stories of God's Quiet Work in a Changing China* (UK: Paternoster Press).

Testimonies of Chinese Christians, helping show the breadth of the Chinese Church.

Yun, Brother with Paul Hattaway
2002 *The Heavenly Man* (London: Monarch Books).

Extraordinary story of a leader in the unregistered churches.

WEB SITES AND OTHER FREE SOURCES

A selection of web sites and other resources—particularly those that give general information, not simply about their own ministry.

China Source is an (American) multi-agency effort 'to provide an up-to-date and accurate analysis of the issues and opportunities facing Christians involved in China service.' They produce a quarterly newsletter (for which you have to pay) and a website.
www.chsource.org

OMF International—the former China Inland Mission—has an excellent suite of resources for learning about, praying for, and serving in China—books, leaflets, newsletters, prayer tapes and conferences.
www.omf.org

Open Doors, an agency which helps the persecuted Church worldwide, hosted seven years of prayer for the Church in the Communist world which ended with the fall of the Berlin Wall. Then they started on ten years of prayer for breakthrough in the Islamic world, which ended around September 11th 2001. From 2002 they are hosting seven years of prayer for China.
www.opendoorsuk.org

Antioch Ministries/Chinese Church Support Ministries. An agency that supports Chinese Christianity in a variety of ways.
www.am-ccsm.org/

China for Jesus claims to be a voice of a grouping of six mainland Chinese house-church networks.
www.chinaforjesus.com

Asia Harvest. Profiles of all China's minorities and much other useful stuff from a ministry that is very well-connected to the house-church movement.
www.asiaharvest.org

Amity News Service. This is the official news site of the registered Church.
www.amityfoundation.org/ans/home

Human Rights Watch gives regular, detailed reports of the nastier side of Chinese politics.
hrw.org

The Economist website is one of many portals that collect together news and analysis on China, a trawl of recent stories from the web, and further helpful sites.
www.economist.com/countries/China/

The China Population and Information Research Centre's website has a fun feature which shows a second-by-second update of China's population.
www.cpirc.org.cn/eindex.htm

FOR PRAYER

1. For the gospel to spread throughout China: for more evangelists, local and foreign, for more Bibles, for continued opportunities and reponse.

2. For China's Church, that it would mature and be strengthened in every way.

3. For China's leaders, local and national, that they would have integrity and wisdom.

4. For a great multiplication of excellent, holistic, Christian-inspired work among China's neediest groups of people.

5. For China's families and children, that they will be renewed and strengthened by God's power.

6. For foreign Christians living in China, for wisdom and integrity in their contribution to Chinese Christian life.

7. For thousands of Chinese Christians to play a part in carrying the gospel to the Buddhist, Hindu and Muslim worlds, 'back to Jerusalem.'